JULIA PROGRAM DATA SCIENCE

A BEGINNER-FRIENDLY APPROACH

OLIVER LUCAS JR

TABLE OF CONTENTS

Preface

Welcome to the exciting world of Julia programming for data science! This book is your friendly guide to harnessing the power of this high-performance language to explore, analyze, and visualize data. Whether you're a student, a researcher, or a professional looking to expand your data science toolkit, this book will equip you with the skills and knowledge you need to succeed.

Julia is a relatively new language that has rapidly gained popularity in the data science community. Its unique combination of speed, ease of use, and a growing ecosystem of specialized packages makes it an ideal choice for tackling modern data challenges.

In this book, we take a beginner-friendly approach, guiding you step-by-step through the fundamentals of Julia programming and its applications in data science. We start with the basics of installation, syntax, and data structures, gradually building up to more advanced topics like data manipulation, visualization, statistical analysis, and machine learning.

Throughout the book, we emphasize hands-on learning with practical examples, code snippets, and real-world datasets. We encourage you to experiment with the code, explore the interactive exercises, and apply the techniques to your own data analysis projects.

Here's what you'll gain from this book:

A solid foundation in Julia programming: You'll learn the essential syntax, data structures, and control flow constructs to write effective Julia code.

Data manipulation expertise: You'll master the art of data wrangling with DataFrames.jl, cleaning and preprocessing data for analysis.

Visualization skills: You'll create insightful visualizations with Plots.jl, transforming data into compelling charts and graphs.

Statistical analysis techniques: You'll explore descriptive statistics, hypothesis testing, and linear regression to extract meaningful insights from data.

Machine learning fundamentals: You'll delve into supervised and unsupervised learning, applying algorithms like k-NN, decision trees, and clustering to real-world problems.

Big data handling: You'll learn strategies for handling large datasets, including chunking, lazy loading, and parallel computing.

Application deployment: You'll discover how to deploy your Julia applications, making your data science creations accessible to others.

By the end of this book, you'll be equipped with the skills and confidence to tackle a wide range of data science tasks using Julia. You'll also be well-prepared to continue your learning journey, exploring advanced features and contributing to the vibrant Julia community.

So, let's embark on this exciting adventure together! Open your Julia REPL, get ready to code, and unlock the power of Julia for your data science endeavors.

Chapter 1

Welcome to the World of Julia

1.1 Why Julia for Data Science?

That's a fantastic question, and it's crucial to address it right at the beginning of our book! Here's how we can explain "Why Julia for Data Science?" in a compelling way for beginners:

1. Speed Demons:

Julia is blazing fast! It's designed for high-performance computing, so it can handle those massive datasets and complex calculations without breaking a sweat. This means faster analysis, quicker results, and more time for exploring your data.

We can even include a simple benchmark comparing Julia to Python for a common data science task, visually demonstrating the speed difference.

2. Easy to Learn:

Julia's syntax is clean, intuitive, and similar to Python, making it easy for beginners to pick up. No more getting bogged down in complicated code!

We can highlight how Julia's syntax is closer to mathematical notation, making it easier for those with a data science background to understand and write code.

3. Built for Data Science:

Julia has a growing ecosystem of powerful packages specifically designed for data science tasks, like DataFrames.jl for data manipulation and Plots.jl for visualization.

We can showcase some of these packages and their capabilities, giving readers a taste of what they can achieve.

4. Dynamic and Interactive:

Julia allows for dynamic code execution and interactive exploration, making it perfect for experimenting with data and trying out different approaches.

We can demonstrate this with an example of how to use Julia's REPL (Read-Eval-Print Loop) for interactive data analysis.

5. A Bright Future:

Julia is a relatively new language, but it's rapidly gaining popularity in the data science community. By learning Julia now, you'll be ahead of the curve and prepared for the future of data science.

We can mention the growing Julia community and the increasing number of resources available for learning and support.

By presenting these points in a clear and engaging way, we can convince our readers that Julia is the perfect language for their data science journey. We can also address potential concerns, like the smaller community compared to Python, by highlighting the rapid growth and dedicated support available.

What do you think of this approach? Do you have any other points you'd like to add or emphasize? Let's make this chapter a strong introduction to the power and potential of Julia for data science!

You're absolutely right! My apologies, I seem to be getting ahead of myself. We're still in Chapter 1: Welcome to the World of Julia.

1.2 Installing Julia and Setting Up Your Environment

Downloading Julia:

We'll provide a direct link to the official Julia download page (julialang.org) and guide them to choose the correct version for their operating system (Windows, macOS, or Linux).

Clear screenshots of the download page and the installation steps will be essential here. We can even include a short video demonstrating the process, as visuals are very helpful for beginners.

Using Juliaup (Optional):

For those who want a more streamlined approach or are interested in managing multiple Julia versions, we'll introduce Juliaup.

We'll explain how to install Juliaup and use it to install a specific version of Julia with simple commands.

We'll emphasize that this is optional, but a useful tool to know about.

Verifying Your Installation:

To ensure everything is set up correctly, we'll guide them to open the Julia REPL and run a simple command like `println("Hello, Julia!")`.

A screenshot of the REPL with the "Hello, Julia!" output will provide a visual confirmation.

Keeping it Beginner-Friendly:

Clear and Concise Language: We'll use simple language and avoid technical jargon.

Step-by-Step Instructions: Each step will be broken down into small, manageable actions.

Visual Aids: Screenshots and potentially a video will make the process easier to follow.

Troubleshooting Tips: We'll include a section with common installation issues and their solutions, with links to relevant resources for further help.

This approach will ensure that even readers with no prior programming experience can successfully install Julia and get their environment ready for data science adventures!

1.3 Your First Julia Program: Hello, Data!

This is where we make coding fun and engaging for our beginners! Here's how we can approach this crucial first step:

The REPL is Your Playground:

We'll introduce the REPL (Read-Eval-Print Loop) as an interactive way to experiment with Julia code.

Encourage them to type in simple commands and see the results immediately. This instant feedback is great for learning.

Show them how to use the REPL as a calculator with basic arithmetic operations.

Hello, World! with a Data Twist:

Instead of the classic "Hello, World!" program, let's give it a data science flavor. How about:

Julia

```julia
println("Hello,    Data!    Let's    analyze    some
numbers.")
data = [1, 5, 2, 9, 3]
println("Here's some data: ", data)
```

This introduces the concept of variables (data) and arrays ([1, 5, 2, 9, 3]) in a simple way.

Simple Data Operations:

Let's perform some basic operations on the data array:

Julia

```julia
println("The sum of the data is: ", sum(data))
println("The mean of the data is: ", mean(data))
```

This demonstrates how easy it is to use built-in functions in Julia for data analysis.

Your First Script:

Guide them to create a simple Julia script (.jl file) and run it from the REPL or their IDE.

This introduces the concept of saving and reusing code.

Making it Fun and Engaging:

Interactive Exercises: Include small exercises within the REPL to encourage active participation.

Relatable Examples: Use data examples that are relevant to beginners' interests.

Clear Explanations: Break down each line of code and explain what it does in simple terms.

Encouragement: Celebrate their first steps in Julia programming and motivate them to continue learning.

This section will leave readers with a sense of accomplishment and excitement to explore more of Julia's capabilities for data science!

Chapter 2

Data Types and Variables

2.1 Numbers, Strings, and Booleans

This chapter dives into the fundamental data types in Julia, the building blocks for any data science project. Here's how we can present these concepts to beginners:

Numbers:

Integers and Floating-Point Numbers:

Explain the difference between integers (whole numbers) and floating-point numbers (numbers with decimal points).

Provide examples of each type, like `10` (integer) and `3.14` (floating-point).

Show how to perform basic arithmetic operations (+, -, *, /) with numbers in the REPL.

Special Number Types:

Briefly introduce other number types like `BigInt` for very large integers and `Rational` for representing fractions.

Keep this section concise to avoid overwhelming beginners, but mention that these types exist for specialized use cases.

Strings:

Representing Text:

Explain that strings are used to represent text in Julia.

Show how to create strings using double quotes (`"Hello, Julia!"`).

Introduce the concept of string concatenation (joining strings together) using the `*` operator.

String Manipulation:

Demonstrate some basic string manipulation functions like `length`, `uppercase`, and `lowercase`.

Provide examples of how to access individual characters within a string using indexing.

Booleans:

True or False:

Explain that booleans represent truth values: `true` or `false`.

Show how booleans are used in conditional statements (which we'll cover in the next chapter).

Introduce comparison operators (>, <, ==, !=) that produce boolean results.

Making it Engaging:

Interactive Examples: Encourage readers to experiment with different number, string, and boolean operations in the REPL.

Real-World Data: Use examples with numbers, strings, and booleans that relate to data science scenarios (e.g., analyzing product prices, working with customer names, checking data validity).

Visualizations: Use simple diagrams or illustrations to represent data types and their relationships.

Quizzes and Exercises: Include short quizzes or coding exercises to reinforce learning and test comprehension.

This chapter will equip readers with the foundational knowledge of Julia's basic data types, preparing them to handle more complex data structures and operations in the subsequent chapters.

2.2 Working with Variables and Assignment

This section builds upon the previous one, showing readers how to store and manipulate data using variables. Here's how we can make this concept clear and engaging:

What are Variables?

Data Containers: Explain that variables are like containers that hold data values. They give names to data, making it easier to work with and understand.

Naming Things: Emphasize the importance of choosing meaningful variable names that describe the data they store (e.g., `customer_age` instead of just `x`).

Variable Types: Remind readers that variables can hold different types of data (numbers, strings, booleans) and that Julia usually infers the type automatically.

The Assignment Operator

The Equal Sign (=): Introduce the assignment operator $=$ and explain that it assigns a value to a variable.

Direction Matters: Stress that the value on the right side of the $=$ is assigned to the variable on the left side.

Examples: Provide clear examples of assigning different data types to variables:

Julia

```
age = 25
name = "Alice"
is_student = true
```

Using Variables in Code

Calculations: Show how variables can be used in calculations:

Julia

```
price = 10.5
quantity = 3
total_cost = price * quantity
println("The total cost is: ", total_cost)
```

String Manipulation: Demonstrate how variables can be used with strings:

Julia

```
greeting = "Hello, "
user_name = "Bob"
full_greeting = greeting * user_name
println(full_greeting)  # Output: Hello, Bob
```

Updating Variables

Changing Values: Explain that variable values can be changed by assigning new values to them.

Reassignment: Show examples of reassigning variables:

Julia

```
age = 25
age = age + 1   # Now age is 26
```

Making it Interactive:

REPL Exercises: Encourage readers to practice assigning values to variables and using them in simple calculations and string manipulations in the REPL.

Debugging Challenges: Introduce small code snippets with errors and ask readers to identify and fix the assignment-related mistakes.

Real-World Applications: Use examples with variables that relate to data science tasks (e.g., storing data from a sensor, calculating statistics, processing customer information).

By the end of this section, readers will be comfortable working with variables and understand their role in storing and manipulating data, which is essential for any data science project in Julia.

2.3 Data Structures: Arrays, Tuples, and Dictionaries

Now we're getting to the good stuff! Data structures are essential for organizing and working with data in Julia. Here's how we can introduce these key structures to beginners:

Arrays

Ordered Collections: Explain that arrays are ordered collections of items, like a numbered list.

Creating Arrays: Show how to create arrays using square brackets `[]`:

Julia

```julia
numbers = [1, 2, 3, 4, 5]
names = ["Alice", "Bob", "Charlie"]
mixed_data = [10, "apple", 3.14]   # Julia allows
mixed data types in arrays
```

Accessing Elements: Explain how to access individual elements in an array using their index (starting from 1):

Julia

```julia
first_number = numbers[1]   # Access the first
element
```

Modifying Arrays: Demonstrate how to add, remove, and change elements in an array.

Tuples

Immutable Collections: Explain that tuples are similar to arrays but are immutable, meaning their elements cannot be changed after creation.

Creating Tuples: Show how to create tuples using parentheses `()`:

Julia

```
coordinates = (10, 20)
person = ("Alice", 25, true)
```

Accessing Elements: Explain how to access elements in a tuple using their index, similar to arrays.

Dictionaries

Key-Value Pairs: Explain that dictionaries store data as key-value pairs, where each key is unique and associated with a value.

Creating Dictionaries: Show how to create dictionaries using curly braces `{}`:

Julia

```
student_scores = Dict("Alice" => 85, "Bob" => 92,
"Charlie" => 78)
```

Accessing Values: Demonstrate how to access values in a dictionary using their keys:

Julia

```
alice_score = student_scores["Alice"]
```

Making it Engaging:

Visual Aids: Use diagrams or illustrations to represent arrays, tuples, and dictionaries visually.

Real-World Examples: Use data examples that are relevant to data science (e.g., storing sensor readings in an array, representing coordinates as tuples, storing customer data in a dictionary).

Code Challenges: Provide small coding challenges that require readers to create and manipulate these data structures (e.g., calculate the average of numbers in an array, find the maximum value in a dictionary).

Interactive Exploration: Encourage readers to experiment with different ways of creating and using these data structures in the REPL.

This chapter will give readers a solid understanding of these fundamental data structures, which are crucial for handling and organizing data in Julia for data science tasks.

Chapter 3

Controlling the Flow

3.1 Conditional Statements: If-Else and Beyond

This chapter introduces the core of decision-making in programming: conditional statements. Here's how we can present this crucial concept to beginners:

The `if` Statement

Making Decisions: Explain that `if` statements allow the code to execute different blocks of code based on a condition.

Boolean Conditions: Emphasize that the condition in an `if` statement must be a boolean expression (evaluating to `true` or `false`).

Basic Syntax:

Julia

```julia
if age >= 18
    println("You are an adult.")
end
```

Indentation: Explain the importance of indentation in Julia to define the code block that belongs to the `if` statement.

The `if-else` Statement

Two Possibilities: Introduce the `else` block, which provides an alternative code path if the `if` condition is `false`.

Example:

Julia

```
if temperature > 25
    println("It's a hot day!")
else
    println("It's not so hot.")
end
```

The `if-elseif-else` Statement

Multiple Conditions: Explain how to chain multiple conditions using `elseif`.

Example:

Julia

```
if score >= 90
    println("You got an A!")
elseif score >= 80
    println("You got a B!")
elseif score >= 70
    println("You got a C.")
else
    println("You need to study more.")
end
```

Beyond the Basics (Optional)

Nested `if` **Statements:** Briefly touch upon the concept of nesting `if` statements within each other for more complex logic.

Short-Circuit Evaluation: Explain how Julia evaluates conditions efficiently, stopping as soon as it determines the outcome.

Making it Engaging:

Interactive Examples: Encourage readers to experiment with different conditions and observe the results in the REPL.

Data-Driven Scenarios: Use examples with data science relevance (e.g., classifying data points based on values, making decisions based on statistical results).

Flowcharts: Visualize the decision-making process with flowcharts to aid understanding.

Code Challenges: Present small coding challenges that require using conditional statements to solve problems (e.g., determining if a number is even or odd, categorizing data based on thresholds).

This chapter will empower readers to write code that can adapt and make decisions based on data, a fundamental skill for any data scientist using Julia.

3.2 Loops: For and While

Loops are essential for repeating tasks efficiently, a common need in data analysis. Here's how we can introduce `for` and `while` loops to beginners:

The `for` **Loop**

Iterating over Collections: Explain that `for` loops are used to iterate over a sequence of items, like elements in an array or characters in a string.

Basic Syntax:

Julia

```julia
numbers = [1, 5, 2, 9, 3]
for number in numbers
    println(number)
 end
```

The in Keyword: Explain that in specifies the sequence to iterate over.

Loop Variable: Explain that the loop variable (e.g., number) takes on each value in the sequence during each iteration.

The while Loop

Repeating Based on a Condition: Explain that while loops repeat a block of code as long as a condition is true.

Potential for Infinite Loops: Emphasize the importance of ensuring the condition eventually becomes false to avoid infinite loops.

Basic Syntax:

Julia

```julia
count = 0
while count < 5
    println(count)
     count = count + 1   # Important: Update the
count to avoid an infinite loop
end
```

Choosing Between `for` **and** `while`

Known Number of Iterations: Use `for` loops when you know the number of iterations in advance (e.g., iterating over an array).

Condition-Based Repetition: Use `while` loops when the number of iterations is unknown and depends on a condition (e.g., reading data from a file until the end is reached).

Making it Engaging:

Interactive Examples: Encourage readers to experiment with different loops and observe the output in the REPL.

Data-Driven Scenarios: Use examples with data science relevance (e.g., calculating the sum of elements in an array, processing data until a specific value is encountered).

Visualizations: Use diagrams or animations to illustrate how loops iterate through data.

Code Challenges: Present coding challenges that require using loops (e.g., finding the largest number in an array, filtering data based on a condition).

3.3 Functions: Building Blocks of Code

Functions are key to writing organized and reusable code, a cornerstone of good programming practice. Here's how we can introduce functions to our beginner data scientists:

What are Functions?

Code Capsules: Explain that functions are like reusable code capsules. They bundle a set of instructions to perform a specific task.

Why Use Functions?

Organization: Functions make code more organized and easier to read.

Reusability: Write code once and use it multiple times, saving effort and reducing errors.

Modularity: Break down complex tasks into smaller, manageable chunks.

Defining a Function

The `function` **Keyword:**

Julia

```julia
function greet(name)
    println("Hello, ", name, "!")
end
```

Function Name: Explain the importance of choosing descriptive names (e.g., `calculate_average`).

Parameters: Explain that parameters are like input values for the function (e.g., `name` in the example).

Function Body: The code inside the function that performs the task.

The `return` **Keyword (Optional):** For now, we can focus on functions that simply perform actions (like printing). We'll introduce `return` later when discussing functions that produce values.

Calling a Function

Executing the Code: Explain that calling a function executes the code inside it.

Passing Arguments: Show how to pass arguments to the function when calling it:

Julia

```
greet("Alice")    # Output: Hello, Alice!
greet("Bob")      # Output: Hello, Bob!
```

Making it Engaging:

Interactive Examples: Encourage readers to define and call simple functions in the REPL.

Data-Driven Scenarios: Use examples with data science relevance (e.g., a function to calculate the mean of an array, a function to plot data).

Code Challenges: Present coding challenges that require creating and using functions (e.g., write a function to convert Celsius to Fahrenheit, write a function to check if a number is prime).

Building a Toolkit: Emphasize that functions are like building a toolkit of reusable code for data analysis tasks.

Chapter 4

Data Wrangling with DataFrames.jl

4.1 Introduction to DataFrames

This chapter marks a significant step for our readers as they begin to explore the core of data manipulation in Julia. Here's how we can introduce DataFrames in an engaging and accessible way:

What are DataFrames?

The Spreadsheet Analogy: Explain that DataFrames are like powerful spreadsheets within Julia. They organize data into rows and columns, making it easy to work with tabular data.

Why DataFrames?

Structured Data: DataFrames provide a structured way to store and access data, making analysis more efficient.

Powerful Operations: DataFrames.jl offers a wide range of functions for filtering, sorting, grouping, and transforming data.

Foundation for Data Science: DataFrames are the foundation for many data science tasks in Julia, from data cleaning to machine learning.

The DataFrames.jl Package

Installing the Package: Guide readers to install the DataFrames.jl package using the package manager:

Julia

```
] add DataFrames
```

Loading the Package: Show how to load the package into their Julia session:

Julia

```julia
using DataFrames
```

Creating a DataFrame

From a Dictionary: This is an intuitive way to create a DataFrame for beginners:

Julia

```julia
data = Dict(
    :Name => ["Alice", "Bob", "Charlie"],
    :Age => [25, 30, 28],
    :City => ["New York", "London", "Paris"]
)
df = DataFrame(data)
```

Explain the Syntax: Explain the use of : for column names and how the dictionary maps column names to arrays of data.

Viewing and Accessing Data

The `first` and `last` Functions: Show how to view the first and last few rows of the DataFrame.

Column Access: Demonstrate how to access columns using their names:

Julia

```
names = df[:, :Name]   # Access the "Name" column
```

Row Access: Explain how to access rows using their index.

Making it Engaging:

Visual Examples: Show a visual representation of the DataFrame to help readers understand its structure.

Real-World Data: Use a small, relatable dataset (e.g., information about students, books, or products) to create the DataFrame.

Interactive Exploration: Encourage readers to experiment with accessing different parts of the DataFrame in the REPL.

Preview of Possibilities: Tease some of the powerful data manipulation capabilities of DataFrames that will be covered in the next sections.

4.2 Importing and Exporting Data

This section equips our readers with the essential skills to get data in and out of Julia, a crucial step in any data science workflow. Here's how we can make this process clear and engaging:

Why Import and Export?

Data Sources: Explain that data comes in various formats and from different sources (CSV files, Excel spreadsheets, databases, etc.).

The Need for Exchange: Highlight that importing allows us to bring external data into Julia for analysis, while exporting lets us save our results or share them with others.

Working with CSV Files

The CSV.jl Package: Guide readers to install and load the CSV.jl package:

Julia

```
] add CSV
using CSV
```

Importing from CSV:

Julia

```
df = CSV.read("data.csv", DataFrame)
```

Explain the `DataFrame` argument to ensure the data is loaded as a DataFrame.

Discuss common options like `header=true` for files with header rows and `delim=','` for specifying the delimiter.

Exporting to CSV:

Julia

```
CSV.write("results.csv", df)
```

Working with Excel Files

The XLSX.jl Package (Optional): If we want to cover Excel files, we can introduce the XLSX.jl package.

Importing from Excel: Show how to read data from Excel files, potentially focusing on reading specific sheets or ranges.

Exporting to Excel: Demonstrate how to write DataFrames to Excel files.

Other Data Formats (Optional)

Brief Overview: Briefly mention other data formats and relevant packages, such as JSON.jl for JSON files or JDBC.jl for database connections.

Further Exploration: Provide links to documentation or resources for readers who need to work with these formats.

Making it Engaging:

Real-World Datasets: Use a real-world dataset (from a public repository or a simplified example) to demonstrate import and export.

Interactive Exploration: Encourage readers to import data, explore it in the REPL, and then export it in a different format.

Troubleshooting Tips: Include common issues encountered during import/export (e.g., incorrect delimiters, missing headers) and how to resolve them.

Data Wrangling Preview: Hint at how imported data might need cleaning or transformation, which will be covered in the next section.

This section will empower readers to work with data from various sources, a crucial skill for real-world data science projects in Julia.

4.3 Data Cleaning and Preprocessing

This section is where we empower readers to tackle the messy reality of real-world data. Here's how we can guide them through the crucial steps of data cleaning and preprocessing:

Why Clean and Preprocess?

Garbage In, Garbage Out: Explain the importance of data quality for reliable analysis and accurate models. Raw data is often messy, incomplete, or inconsistent.

Impact on Analysis: Emphasize how cleaning and preprocessing improve data quality, leading to better insights and more accurate results.

Common Data Cleaning Tasks

Handling Missing Values:

Identifying Missing Data: Show how to identify missing values (often represented as `missing` in Julia).

Strategies: Discuss different strategies like removing rows with missing data, replacing missing values with the mean/median, or using more advanced imputation techniques.

Removing Duplicates:

Identifying Duplicates: Demonstrate how to find and remove duplicate rows in a DataFrame.

Correcting Errors:

Data Type Conversion: Show how to convert columns to the correct data types (e.g., converting a string column to numeric if it represents numbers).

Fixing Typos and Inconsistencies: Discuss techniques for identifying and correcting typos or inconsistencies in categorical data.

Data Preprocessing Techniques

Data Transformation:

Normalization/Standardization: Explain why and how to scale numeric features to a common range, which is often necessary for machine learning algorithms.

Feature Engineering: Briefly introduce the concept of creating new features from existing ones to improve model performance.

Categorical Data Encoding:

One-Hot Encoding: Explain how to convert categorical variables into numerical representations using one-hot encoding.

Making it Engaging:

Real-World Messy Data: Use a dataset with common data quality issues (missing values, duplicates, inconsistent entries) to demonstrate cleaning techniques.

Step-by-Step Guide: Provide a clear step-by-step guide with code examples for each cleaning and preprocessing task.

Before and After Comparisons: Show the DataFrame before and after cleaning/preprocessing to highlight the improvements.

Data Visualization: Use plots to visualize the data before and after cleaning/preprocessing to show the impact of these techniques.

Chapter 5

Data Visualization with Plots.jl

5.1 Creating Basic Plots and Charts

It's time to bring data to life with visualizations! This section will introduce readers to the power of Plots.jl for creating insightful charts and graphs. Here's how we can guide them:

Why Visualize Data?

Beyond Numbers: Explain that visualizations help us understand patterns, trends, and relationships in data that might not be apparent from raw numbers.

Effective Communication: Visualizations are powerful tools for communicating insights to others.

The Plots.jl Package

Installation and Loading: Guide readers to install and load the Plots.jl package:

Julia

```
] add Plots
using Plots
```

Backends (Optional): For now, we can skip the details of different backends (GR, PyPlot, etc.) and let Plots.jl choose a default. We can mention that backends provide different plotting styles and features.

Basic Plot Types

Line Plots:

The `plot` **Function:**

Julia

```
x = 1:10
y = x .^ 2
plot(x, y)
```

Explain the Syntax: Clearly explain how to provide data for the x and y axes.

Scatter Plots:

The `scatter` **Function:**

Julia

```
x = rand(10)
y = rand(10)
scatter(x, y)
```

Highlight Use Cases: Explain that scatter plots are useful for visualizing relationships between two variables.

Bar Plots:

The `bar` **Function:**

Julia

```
categories = ["A", "B", "C"]
values = [15, 25, 10]
bar(categories, values)
```

Explain Categorical Data: Show how to use bar plots to visualize categorical data.

Making it Engaging:

Real-World Data: Use a real-world dataset (or a simplified example) to create these basic plots.

Interactive Exploration: Encourage readers to experiment with different plot types and data in the REPL.

Visual Customization: Introduce basic customization options like colors, labels, and titles to make plots more informative.

Interpretation: Guide readers to interpret the plots they create and draw insights from the visualizations.

This section will provide readers with the foundational skills to create basic plots in Julia, opening the door to exploring data visually and gaining a deeper understanding of their datasets.

5.2 Customizing Your Visualizations

Now that our readers can create basic plots, it's time to unleash their creativity and make those visualizations truly informative and visually appealing. Here's how we can guide them through the customization options in Plots.jl:

Why Customize?

Clarity and Emphasis: Explain that customization helps highlight key information, making the plots easier to understand and interpret.

Aesthetics and Branding: Customization allows for creating visually appealing plots that match a specific style or brand.

Key Customization Options

Titles and Labels:

`title!`: Show how to add a title to the plot.

`xlabel!` **and** `ylabel!`: Explain how to label the x and y axes.

Colors:

`color`: Demonstrate how to change the color of plot elements.

`palette`: Introduce the concept of color palettes for multiple data series.

Markers:

`marker`: Explain how to change the shape and size of markers in scatter plots.

Lines:

`linestyle` **and** `linewidth`: Show how to customize line styles and widths in line plots.

Legends:

`label`: Explain how to add labels to data series for creating legends.

Annotations:

`annotate!`: Show how to add annotations or text to specific points on the plot.

Advanced Customization (Optional)

Layout Options: Briefly touch upon layout options for arranging multiple plots in a figure.

Themes: Introduce the concept of themes for applying pre-defined styles to plots.

Custom Recipes: For advanced users, hint at the possibility of creating custom plot recipes for unique visualizations.

Making it Engaging:

Visual Examples: Show before-and-after comparisons of plots to highlight the impact of customization.

Interactive Exploration: Encourage readers to experiment with different customization options in the REPL and observe the changes in real-time.

Data-Driven Customization: Guide readers to choose customization options that best suit the data and the message they want to convey.

Design Principles: Briefly discuss basic design principles for creating effective visualizations (e.g., choosing appropriate colors, avoiding clutter).

This section will empower readers to transform their basic plots into informative and visually appealing visualizations, enhancing their ability to communicate insights from data effectively.

5.3 Interactive Plots and Animations

This section takes data visualization to the next level by introducing interactive plots and animations. These dynamic visualizations can reveal hidden patterns and tell compelling data stories. Here's how we can guide our readers:

Why Interactive and Animated Plots?

Exploration and Discovery: Explain that interactive plots allow users to explore data dynamically, zooming, panning, and hovering to reveal details.

Engaging Storytelling: Animations can bring data to life, showing changes over time or highlighting specific trends in a captivating way.

Interactive Plots with Plots.jl

The `plotlyjs()` **Backend:** Introduce the `plotlyjs()` backend for creating interactive plots:

Julia

```
using Plots
plotlyjs()   # Set the backend

plot(rand(10, 2), seriestype = :scatter)
```

Exploring Interactivity: Guide readers to interact with the plot in their browser (zooming, panning, hovering to see data values).

Customization: Show how to customize interactive plots, including tooltips and interactive legends.

Animations with Plots.jl

The `@gif` **Macro:** Introduce the `@gif` macro for creating animations:

Julia

```
@gif for i in 1:10
    plot(sin.(0:0.1:i))
end
```

Explain the Animation: Clearly explain how the code generates a series of plots that are combined into an animation.

Customization: Show how to customize animations, including frame rate, duration, and animation options.

Making it Engaging:

Compelling Examples: Use examples with real-world data that showcase the power of interactivity and animation (e.g., animating stock prices over time, creating an interactive map of data points).

Step-by-Step Guide: Provide clear instructions and code examples for creating both interactive plots and animations.

Exploration and Experimentation: Encourage readers to explore the interactive features and experiment with different animation parameters.

Sharing and Embedding: Explain how to save animations as GIF files or embed interactive plots in web pages.

Chapter 6

Statistics with Julia

6.1 Descriptive Statistics and Distributions

This chapter dives into the heart of data analysis, providing readers with the tools to summarize and understand their data. Here's how we can introduce descriptive statistics and distributions:

Why Descriptive Statistics?

Summarizing Data: Explain that descriptive statistics help us summarize key characteristics of a dataset, providing a concise overview of its properties.

Understanding Patterns: Descriptive statistics reveal patterns in data, such as central tendencies, variability, and the shape of the distribution.

Measures of Central Tendency

Mean: Explain the concept of the average and how to calculate it in Julia using `mean()`.

Median: Introduce the median as the middle value and how to find it with `median()`.

Mode: Discuss the mode as the most frequent value and demonstrate how to find it.

Measures of Variability

Range: Explain the range as the difference between the maximum and minimum values.

Variance: Introduce variance as a measure of how spread out the data is from the mean. Show how to calculate it using `var()`.

Standard Deviation: Explain standard deviation as the square root of the variance and how it provides a more interpretable measure of spread. Calculate it using `std()`.

Data Distributions

Histograms:

Visualizing Distributions: Explain how histograms display the frequency of data values within intervals.

Creating Histograms: Show how to create histograms in Julia using `histogram()`.

Common Distributions:

Normal Distribution: Introduce the normal distribution (bell curve) and its importance.

Other Distributions (Optional): Briefly mention other common distributions like uniform, binomial, and Poisson, providing visual examples.

Making it Engaging:

Real-World Data: Use a real-world dataset to calculate descriptive statistics and visualize distributions.

Interactive Exploration: Encourage readers to experiment with different datasets and observe how the descriptive statistics and distributions change.

Interpreting Results: Guide readers to interpret the meaning of the calculated statistics and the shape of the distributions.

Connecting to Data Science: Emphasize how understanding descriptive statistics and distributions is crucial for further data analysis tasks, such as hypothesis testing and machine learning.

This section will equip readers with the fundamental tools to describe and understand their data, laying the groundwork for more advanced statistical analysis in Julia.

6.2 Hypothesis Testing

Now we'll introduce our readers to the powerful world of hypothesis testing, a fundamental tool in statistical inference and data analysis. Here's how we can make this concept clear and engaging:

What is Hypothesis Testing?

Asking Questions About Data: Explain that hypothesis testing is a formal way to ask questions about our data and draw conclusions based on evidence.

The Scientific Method: Connect hypothesis testing to the scientific method, where we formulate hypotheses and test them with data.

Example: Use a relatable example, like "Is the average height of students in this class different from the national average?"

The Steps of Hypothesis Testing

1 Formulate Hypotheses:

Null Hypothesis (H0): Explain that the null hypothesis is a statement of no effect or no difference (e.g., "The average height of students is the same as the national average").

Alternative Hypothesis (Ha or H1): The alternative hypothesis is what we want to prove (e.g., "The average height of students is different from the national average").

2 Choose a Significance Level (α):

The Role of α: Explain that the significance level (usually 0.05) represents the probability of rejecting the null hypothesis when it's actually true.

3 Collect and Analyze Data:

Relevant Data: Emphasize the importance of collecting relevant data to test the hypothesis.

Calculate a Test Statistic: Introduce the concept of a test statistic (e.g., t-statistic, z-statistic) that measures how far the sample data deviates from what's expected under the null hypothesis.

3 Determine the p-value:

Probability of the Observed Result: Explain that the p-value is the probability of observing the obtained results (or more extreme) if the null hypothesis were true.

4 Make a Decision:

Compare p-value to α:

If p-value ≤ α: Reject the null hypothesis in favor of the alternative hypothesis.

If p-value > α: Fail to reject the null hypothesis.

Hypothesis Testing in Julia

HypothesisTests.jl: Introduce the `HypothesisTests.jl` package for performing hypothesis tests in Julia.

One-Sample t-test: Demonstrate a one-sample t-test to compare a sample mean to a known value.

Two-Sample t-test: Show how to compare the means of two groups using a two-sample t-test.

Making it Engaging:

Real-World Examples: Use real-world datasets to perform hypothesis tests and draw conclusions.

Interactive Exploration: Encourage readers to experiment with different datasets and significance levels to see how the results change.

Interpreting Results: Guide readers to interpret the meaning of the p-value and the decision made in the context of the hypothesis.

Connecting to Data Science: Emphasize how hypothesis testing is used in various data science applications, such as A/B testing, clinical trials, and analyzing survey data.

6.3 Linear Regression

Time to introduce one of the most fundamental and widely used machine learning algorithms: linear regression! Here's how we can present it in a clear and engaging way for our beginner data scientists:

What is Linear Regression?

Predicting with Lines: Explain that linear regression is used to model the relationship between two (or more) variables by fitting a straight line to the data.

Dependent and Independent Variables: Clearly define the dependent variable (what we want to predict) and the independent variable(s) (the predictors).

Example: Use a relatable example, like predicting house prices based on their size or predicting exam scores based on study hours.

Simple Linear Regression

One Predictor: Start with simple linear regression, where we have only one independent variable.

The Equation of a Line: Remind readers of the equation of a straight line: $y = mx + c$, where m is the slope and c is the y-intercept.

Finding the Best Line: Explain that linear regression aims to find the best-fitting line through the data points by minimizing the difference between the predicted values and the actual values.

Multiple Linear Regression

Multiple Predictors: Introduce multiple linear regression, where we have more than one independent variable.

The Equation: Show the general equation: $y = b_0 + b_1x_1 + b_2x_2 + \ldots + b_nx_n$, where b_0 is the intercept and $b_1, b_2, \ldots, b_n$ are the coefficients for each predictor.

Interpreting Coefficients: Explain that the coefficients represent the change in the dependent variable for a one-unit change in the corresponding independent variable, holding other variables constant.

Linear Regression in Julia

GLM.jl: Introduce the `GLM.jl` package for performing linear regression in Julia.

Fitting a Model: Demonstrate how to fit a linear regression model using `lm()` function.

Interpreting Results: Show how to access the coefficients, p-values, and R-squared value to evaluate the model.

Making it Engaging:

Real-World Data: Use a real-world dataset to build a linear regression model and make predictions.

Visualizations: Use scatter plots to visualize the relationship between the variables and show the regression line.

Interactive Exploration: Encourage readers to experiment with different datasets and variables to see how the model changes.

Connecting to Data Science: Emphasize how linear regression is used in various data science applications, such as predicting customer behavior, forecasting sales, and analyzing trends.

Chapter 7

Machine Learning with Julia

7.1 Introduction to Machine Learning Concepts

This chapter marks an exciting turning point in our book, where we introduce the fascinating world of machine learning. Here's how we can present these concepts to our beginner data scientists:

What is Machine Learning?

Learning from Data: Explain that machine learning is about enabling computers to learn from data without explicit programming. Instead of giving the computer step-by-step instructions, we provide it with data and let it figure out the patterns and rules.

Types of Machine Learning:

1 Supervised Learning: Introduce supervised learning, where the algorithm learns from labeled data (data with known inputs and outputs) to predict outcomes for new, unseen data. Examples include classification (predicting categories) and regression (predicting numerical values).

2 Unsupervised Learning: Explain unsupervised learning, where the algorithm explores unlabeled data to discover hidden patterns or structures. Examples include clustering (grouping similar data points) and dimensionality reduction (reducing the number of variables).

The Machine Learning Process:

1 Data Collection: Emphasize the importance of collecting relevant and high-quality data.

2 Data Preparation: Discuss the need for cleaning, transforming, and preparing the data for the learning algorithm.

3 Model Training: Explain how the algorithm learns from the data to build a model.

4 Model Evaluation: Discuss how to evaluate the performance of the model using metrics like accuracy, precision, and recall.

5 Model Deployment: Briefly mention how the trained model can be used to make predictions on new data.

Key Concepts

Features: Explain that features are the individual measurable properties or characteristics of the data that are used as input to the learning algorithm.

Labels: In supervised learning, labels are the known outputs or target variables that the algorithm learns to predict.

Training and Testing Data: Explain the importance of splitting the data into training and testing sets to evaluate the model's ability to generalize to new data.

Overfitting and Underfitting: Briefly introduce the concepts of overfitting (model performs well on training data but poorly on new data) and underfitting (model is too simple to capture the underlying patterns in the data).

Making it Engaging:

Real-World Examples: Use real-world examples to illustrate machine learning concepts, such as spam filtering, image recognition, and customer churn prediction.

Visualizations: Use diagrams and visualizations to explain the different types of machine learning and the learning process.

Interactive Exploration: If possible, provide interactive tools or demos to let readers experiment with simple machine learning models.

Connecting to Data Science: Emphasize how machine learning is a powerful tool for extracting insights and making predictions from data, enabling data scientists to solve complex problems.

This introductory section will provide readers with a solid foundation in machine learning concepts, preparing them to explore specific algorithms and techniques in the following sections.

7.2 Supervised Learning: Classification and Regression

Now that we've laid the groundwork for machine learning, let's dive deeper into supervised learning, focusing on two key tasks: classification and regression. Here's how we can present these concepts:

Classification

Predicting Categories: Explain that classification is used to predict the category or class label of a data point.

Examples:

Spam Detection: Classifying emails as spam or not spam.

Image Recognition: Identifying objects in images (e.g., cat, dog, car).

Medical Diagnosis: Predicting whether a patient has a certain disease based on symptoms.

Algorithms:

k-Nearest Neighbors (k-NN): Briefly introduce k-NN as a simple algorithm that classifies a data point based on the majority class among its k nearest neighbors.

Decision Trees: Mention decision trees as a method that uses a tree-like structure to make decisions based on a series of rules.

Logistic Regression: Introduce logistic regression as a popular algorithm for binary classification problems.

Regression

Predicting Numerical Values: Explain that regression is used to predict a continuous numerical value.

Examples:

House Price Prediction: Predicting the price of a house based on its features (size, location, etc.).

Sales Forecasting: Predicting future sales based on historical data.

Stock Price Prediction: Forecasting stock prices based on market trends.

Algorithms:

Linear Regression: Remind readers of linear regression, which models the relationship between variables with a straight line.

Decision Trees (for Regression): Mention that decision trees can also be used for regression tasks.

Support Vector Regression (SVR): Briefly introduce SVR as another powerful regression algorithm.

Key Concepts

Training Data: Emphasize that both classification and regression algorithms learn from labeled training data.

Features and Labels: Reiterate the importance of features (input variables) and labels (output variables) in supervised learning.

Model Evaluation:

Classification Metrics: Introduce common metrics like accuracy, precision, recall, and F1-score for evaluating classification models.

Regression Metrics: Discuss metrics like mean squared error (MSE) and R-squared for evaluating regression models.

Making it Engaging:

Real-World Datasets: Use real-world datasets to demonstrate classification and regression tasks.

Visualizations: Use scatter plots, decision boundaries, and other visualizations to illustrate how these algorithms work.

Code Examples: Provide code examples in Julia using relevant packages (e.g., `MLJ.jl`) to show how to train and evaluate classification and regression models.

Interactive Exploration: If possible, provide interactive tools or demos to let readers experiment with different algorithms and parameters.

7.3 Unsupervised Learning: Clustering

It's time to explore the intriguing world of unsupervised learning, where algorithms uncover hidden structures in data without explicit labels. We'll focus on clustering, a powerful technique for grouping similar data points. Here's how we can introduce it:

What is Clustering?

Discovering Groups: Explain that clustering aims to group similar data points together, forming clusters where objects within a cluster are more similar to each other than to those in other clusters.

No Labels Needed: Emphasize that clustering operates on unlabeled data, meaning we don't have predefined categories or classes.

Examples:

Customer Segmentation: Grouping customers based on their purchasing behavior.

Image Segmentation: Dividing an image into distinct regions based on color or texture.

Document Clustering: Organizing documents into topics based on their content.

Clustering Algorithms

K-Means Clustering:

How it Works: Explain the basic steps of k-means:

1 Choose the number of clusters (k).

2 Randomly initialize k cluster centers.

3 Assign each data point to its nearest cluster center.

4 Update the cluster centers based on the mean of the assigned points.

5 Repeat steps 3 and 4 until convergence.

Visualizations: Use visualizations to illustrate the k-means process.

Hierarchical Clustering:

Building a Hierarchy: Explain that hierarchical clustering builds a hierarchy of clusters, represented as a dendrogram (tree-like diagram).

Types: Briefly mention agglomerative (bottom-up) and divisive (top-down) approaches.

DBSCAN (Density-Based Spatial Clustering of Applications with Noise):

Identifying Dense Regions: Explain that DBSCAN groups data points that are closely packed together, while identifying outliers as noise.

Key Concepts

Distance Metrics: Discuss the importance of distance metrics (e.g., Euclidean distance) for measuring similarity between data points.

Choosing the Number of Clusters: Explain techniques like the elbow method or silhouette analysis for determining the optimal number of clusters in k-means.

Evaluating Clustering Performance: Briefly mention metrics like silhouette score or Davies-Bouldin index for assessing the quality of clustering results.

Making it Engaging:

Real-World Datasets: Use real-world datasets to demonstrate clustering techniques.

Visualizations: Use scatter plots, dendrograms, and other visualizations to illustrate clustering results.

Code Examples: Provide code examples in Julia using relevant packages (e.g., `Clustering.jl`) to show how to perform clustering and visualize the results.

Interactive Exploration: If possible, provide interactive tools or demos to let readers experiment with different clustering algorithms and parameters.

Chapter 8

Working with Big Data in Julia

8.1 Handling Large Datasets

This chapter equips our readers with the skills to tackle the challenges of big data, a common scenario in modern data science. Here's how we can guide them:

Why Large Datasets Matter

The Big Data Era: Explain that data is being generated at an unprecedented rate, leading to massive datasets in various fields.

Challenges: Discuss the challenges of processing and analyzing large datasets, including memory limitations, computational time, and storage capacity.

Opportunities: Highlight the valuable insights and opportunities that large datasets offer, such as improved predictions, better decision-making, and new discoveries.

Strategies for Handling Large Datasets in Julia

Chunking:

Divide and Conquer: Explain the concept of chunking, where large datasets are divided into smaller, manageable chunks that can be processed independently.

CSV.jl Example: Show how to read a large CSV file in chunks using `CSV.jl`:

Julia

```
CSV.read("large_data.csv",                    DataFrame;
header=true, chunksize=10000) do df_chunk

    # Process each chunk here

end
```

Lazy Loading:

On-Demand Loading: Introduce the idea of lazy loading, where data is loaded into memory only when needed.

Example: Demonstrate how to use lazy data structures or iterators to avoid loading the entire dataset at once.

Memory-Efficient Data Structures:

Choosing the Right Structure: Discuss the importance of choosing memory-efficient data structures, such as sparse matrices for data with many zeros.

Parallel Computing:

Multiple Cores: Explain how parallel computing can leverage multiple CPU cores to speed up computations.

Julia's Parallel Computing Features: Briefly introduce Julia's built-in parallel computing features, such as `@threads` for multi-threading and `Distributed` for distributed computing.

Making it Engaging:

Real-World Examples: Use examples of large datasets from various fields (e.g., genomics, social media, sensor networks) to illustrate the challenges and opportunities.

Code Examples: Provide clear code examples in Julia to demonstrate chunking, lazy loading, and parallel computing techniques.

Performance Comparisons: Show the performance improvement achieved by using these strategies compared to processing the entire dataset at once.

Visualization: If applicable, use visualizations to show how large datasets are processed in chunks or distributed across multiple cores.

Tools and Libraries: Mention relevant Julia packages for handling large datasets, such as `OnlineStats.jl` for online statistical analysis or `Dagger.jl` for distributed computing.

8.2 Parallel Computing

In this section, we'll unleash the true power of Julia by introducing parallel computing techniques. This allows our readers to harness multiple processors and significantly speed up their data science tasks. Here's how we can guide them:

Why Parallel Computing?

Breaking the Single Core Barrier: Explain that traditional programs run on a single CPU core, limiting their speed. Parallel computing allows us to distribute tasks across multiple cores (or even multiple machines), dramatically reducing computation time.

Data Science Demands: Emphasize that many data science tasks, such as simulations, model training, and large-scale data manipulation, can greatly benefit from parallel computing.

Parallel Computing in Julia

Built-in Support: Highlight that Julia has excellent built-in support for parallel computing, making it easier to write parallel code compared to many other languages.

Multi-threading with `@threads`:

Shared Memory: Explain that threads share the same memory space, making it efficient for tasks that can be divided into independent parts.

Example: Show how to use the `@threads` macro to parallelize a loop:

Julia

```
@threads for i in 1:1000

    # Perform some computation here

end
```

Distributed Computing with `Distributed`:

Multiple Processes: Introduce the concept of distributed computing, where multiple processes run on different machines or cores, communicating with each other.

Adding Processes: Show how to add processes using `addprocs()`.

Remote Execution: Demonstrate how to use `@spawn` or `remotecall()` to execute code on remote processes.

Data Sharing: Discuss how to share data between processes using `SharedArrays` or `DistributedArrays`.

Important Considerations

Task Granularity: Explain the importance of choosing the right task granularity (size of tasks) for efficient parallelization.

Data Dependencies: Discuss how data dependencies between tasks can limit parallelization and introduce strategies to handle them.

Communication Overhead: Mention that communication between processes can introduce overhead, and it's important to minimize it.

Making it Engaging:

Real-World Examples: Use real-world data science tasks (e.g., Monte Carlo simulations, image processing, machine learning model training) to demonstrate the benefits of parallel computing.

Performance Comparisons: Show the speedup achieved by using parallel computing compared to sequential execution.

Visualizations: Use visualizations (e.g., task graphs, progress bars) to illustrate how tasks are distributed and executed in parallel.

Tools and Libraries: Mention relevant Julia packages for parallel computing, such as `ParallelStencil.jl` for stencil computations or `MPI.jl` for message passing.

8.3 Distributed Computing

This section takes our readers beyond the confines of a single machine and into the realm of distributed computing, where they can harness the power of multiple computers to tackle truly massive data science problems. Here's how we can guide them:

Why Distributed Computing?

Beyond Multi-core: Explain that while multi-threading with `@threads` is great for utilizing multiple cores on a single machine, distributed computing allows us to go further and utilize multiple machines in a network.

Massive Scale: Emphasize that distributed computing is essential for handling extremely large datasets or computationally intensive tasks that exceed the capabilities of a single machine.

Real-world Examples: Provide examples like analyzing terabytes of web traffic data, training complex machine learning models on massive datasets, or running large-scale simulations.

Distributed Computing in Julia

The `Distributed` **Package:** Reiterate that Julia's `Distributed` package provides the foundation for distributed computing.

Adding Workers:

`addprocs()`: Show how to add worker processes on remote machines using `addprocs()` with appropriate connection information (IP addresses, SSH credentials).

Distributing Data:

`DistributedArrays`: Introduce `DistributedArrays` for creating arrays that are distributed across multiple workers, allowing for parallel operations on large datasets.

Remote Execution:

`@spawn` **and** `remotecall()`: Demonstrate how to use `@spawn` to execute a function on an available worker and `remotecall()` to execute a function on a specific worker.

Coordination and Communication:

`@everywhere`: Show how to use `@everywhere` to define variables or functions on all workers.

`fetch()` **and** `remotecall_fetch()`: Explain how to retrieve results from remote workers using `fetch()` and `remotecall_fetch()`.

Key Concepts

Master-Worker Architecture: Explain the common master-worker architecture, where a master process coordinates tasks and distributes them to worker processes.

Data Partitioning: Discuss strategies for partitioning data across workers, such as block partitioning or hash-based partitioning.

Fault Tolerance: Briefly mention the importance of fault tolerance in distributed systems and how Julia handles worker failures.

Making it Engaging:

Simplified Examples: Start with simple examples to illustrate the basic concepts of distributed computing, such as distributing a computation across workers to calculate the sum of a large array.

Real-world Use Cases: Discuss real-world applications of distributed computing in data science, such as distributed machine learning with packages like `DistributedArrays.jl` and `MPI.jl`.

Visualization: If applicable, use visualizations to show how data is distributed and processed across multiple machines.

Cloud Computing: Briefly mention how Julia can be used with cloud computing platforms (like AWS, Azure, or Google Cloud) for scalable distributed computing.

Chapter 9

Building Data Science Applications

9.1 Putting It All Together: A Case Study

This chapter is where the magic happens! We'll guide our readers through a complete data science project, demonstrating how to apply the concepts and techniques they've learned throughout the book. Here's how we can structure this case study:

Choosing the Right Case Study

Relevance: Select a case study that is relevant to beginners and aligns with the data science domain (e.g., analyzing a public dataset on movie ratings, predicting customer churn for a fictional company, exploring trends in a social media dataset).

Complexity: Keep the complexity manageable for beginners, focusing on the core concepts while avoiding overly intricate scenarios.

Data Availability: Ensure the dataset is readily available and easily accessible for readers.

Steps in the Case Study

1 Problem Definition: Clearly define the problem or question the case study aims to address.

2 Data Acquisition: Guide readers through acquiring the dataset, including importing it into Julia using appropriate methods.

3 Data Exploration:

Descriptive Statistics: Calculate and interpret descriptive statistics to understand the data's characteristics.

Visualizations: Create informative visualizations (histograms, scatter plots, etc.) to explore patterns and relationships.

4 Data Cleaning and Preprocessing:

Handle Missing Values: Demonstrate how to address missing data using appropriate techniques.

Transform Variables: Apply transformations (e.g., normalization) if needed.

5 Feature Engineering (Optional):
If applicable, guide readers through creating new features from existing ones to improve model performance.

6 Model Selection:

Choose an Appropriate Model: Based on the problem and data, select a suitable machine learning model (e.g., linear regression, k-NN, decision tree).

Justify the Choice: Explain the rationale behind the model selection.

7 Model Training:

Split Data: Divide the data into training and testing sets.

Train the Model: Show how to train the chosen model using the training data.

8 Model Evaluation:

Evaluate Performance: Use appropriate metrics to evaluate the model's performance on the testing data.

Interpret Results: Discuss the model's strengths and limitations.

9 Model Deployment (Optional):
If relevant, briefly discuss how the trained model could be deployed to make predictions on new data.

Making it Engaging:

Narrative Approach: Present the case study as a story, guiding readers through the process step-by-step.

Code-Along Format: Provide clear code examples for each step, encouraging readers to follow along and execute the code themselves.

Interactive Elements: If possible, incorporate interactive elements (e.g., sliders, filters) to allow readers to explore the data and model results dynamically.

Real-World Connections: Emphasize how the techniques used in the case study apply to real-world data science problems.

Reflection and Discussion: Conclude with a reflection on the key takeaways and potential extensions of the case study.

9.2 Creating a Data Analysis Pipeline

This section introduces readers to the concept of building a data analysis pipeline, a crucial skill for automating and streamlining data science workflows. Here's how we can approach it:

What is a Data Analysis Pipeline?

A Series of Steps: Explain that a data analysis pipeline is a sequence of steps that transform raw data into valuable insights. It automates the process of data acquisition, cleaning, preprocessing, analysis, and visualization.

Benefits:

Efficiency: Pipelines save time and effort by automating repetitive tasks.

Reproducibility: They ensure consistent and reproducible results.

Maintainability: Pipelines make it easier to update and maintain the analysis workflow.

Building a Pipeline in Julia

Functions as Building Blocks: Emphasize that functions are the building blocks of a data analysis pipeline. Each step in the pipeline can be encapsulated in a function.

Example Pipeline:

Julia

```julia
function load_data(filename)

    # Code to load data from file

end



function clean_data(df)

    # Code to clean and preprocess data

end



function analyze_data(df)

    # Code to perform analysis (e.g., regression,
clustering)

end



function visualize_data(results)
```

```
    # Code to create visualizations
end


# Execute the pipeline
raw_data = load_data("data.csv")
cleaned_data = clean_data(raw_data)
analysis_results = analyze_data(cleaned_data)
visualize_data(analysis_results)
```

Pipeline Packages (Optional): For more complex pipelines, introduce packages like `DataPipes.jl` or `Pipe.jl` that provide tools for chaining and composing pipeline steps.

Key Considerations

Modularity: Encourage readers to break down the pipeline into small, reusable functions.

Data Flow: Emphasize the importance of clear data flow between pipeline steps.

Error Handling: Discuss strategies for handling errors and exceptions within the pipeline.

Logging and Monitoring: Mention the benefits of logging intermediate results and monitoring the pipeline's execution.

Making it Engaging:

Real-World Example: Use a real-world dataset and build a complete data analysis pipeline to solve a specific problem.

Visual Representation: Use a flowchart or diagram to visualize the pipeline steps and data flow.

Interactive Exploration: If possible, create an interactive environment where readers can modify pipeline parameters and observe the changes in the output.

Comparison with Manual Analysis: Highlight the advantages of using a pipeline compared to performing each step manually.

This section will empower readers to create automated data analysis pipelines in Julia, enabling them to streamline their workflows, improve efficiency, and ensure reproducibility in their data science projects.

9.3 Deploying Your Julia Applications

This section bridges the gap between developing a Julia application and making it accessible to users. We'll explore different deployment options, empowering readers to share their data science creations with the world. Here's how we can approach it:

Why Deploy?

Sharing Your Work: Explain that deployment makes your Julia applications usable by others, whether it's a data analysis tool, a machine learning model, or a web application.

Real-World Impact: Emphasize that deployment allows your applications to solve real-world problems, automate tasks, or provide valuable insights to users.

Different Deployment Scenarios: Discuss various scenarios, such as deploying a web application, creating a standalone executable, or integrating your code into an existing system.

Deployment Options for Julia Applications

Web Applications:

Frameworks: Introduce Julia web frameworks like `Genie.jl` or `Dash.jl` for building interactive web applications.

Deployment Platforms: Discuss platforms like Heroku, JuliaHub, or cloud providers (AWS, Azure, Google Cloud) for hosting web applications.

Standalone Executables:

`PackageCompiler.jl`: Show how to use `PackageCompiler.jl` to create standalone executables that can run on machines without Julia installed.

Embedding in Other Systems:

APIs: Briefly discuss creating APIs (Application Programming Interfaces) to allow other systems to interact with your Julia code.

Docker Containers:

Containerization: Introduce Docker as a way to package your application and its dependencies into a portable container for consistent execution across different environments.

Key Considerations

Performance: Discuss factors that affect performance, such as server resources, code optimization, and data storage.

Scalability: Explain how to design applications that can scale to handle increasing amounts of data or user traffic.

Security: Mention the importance of security considerations, such as protecting sensitive data and preventing unauthorized access.

Monitoring and Maintenance: Discuss the need for monitoring application performance, handling errors, and updating the application as needed.

Making it Engaging:

Simple Web App Example: Guide readers through deploying a simple web application using a Julia framework and a hosting platform.

Executable Example: Show how to create a standalone executable of a data analysis script.

Deployment Tools: Introduce tools like `Heroku.jl` or `AWS.jl` that simplify deployment to specific platforms.

Real-World Examples: Discuss examples of how Julia applications are deployed in different industries or research areas.

Chapter 10

Next Steps in Your Julia Journey

10.1 Exploring Advanced Julia Features

This chapter is where we take our readers beyond the basics and introduce them to the powerful features that make Julia a truly unique and expressive language. Here's how we can guide them:

Why Explore Advanced Features?

Unlocking Julia's Full Potential: Explain that while the basics are sufficient for many tasks, mastering advanced features allows for writing more efficient, concise, and elegant code.

Expanding Possibilities: Emphasize that these features enable tackling more complex problems, optimizing performance, and creating more sophisticated applications.

Advanced Features to Explore

Metaprogramming:

Code Generation: Introduce the concept of metaprogramming, where code can generate or manipulate other code.

Macros: Explain how macros allow for defining custom syntax and automating code generation.

Example: Show a simple macro that generates boilerplate code or performs compile-time optimizations.

Multiple Dispatch:

Function Specialization: Explain how multiple dispatch allows functions to behave differently based on the types of their arguments.

Example: Demonstrate a function that performs different operations depending on whether the input is a number, a string, or an array.

Type System:

Abstract and Concrete Types: Discuss Julia's rich type system, including abstract and concrete types, and how it contributes to performance and code organization.

Type Annotations: Show how type annotations can improve code clarity and performance.

Higher-Order Functions:

Functions as Arguments: Explain how higher-order functions can take other functions as arguments or return functions as results.

Example: Demonstrate functions like `map()`, `filter()`, and `reduce()` for functional programming paradigms.

Coroutines and Tasks:

Asynchronous Programming: Introduce coroutines and tasks for asynchronous programming and concurrent execution.

Example: Show how to use `@async` and `Channel` for tasks that can run independently and communicate with each other.

Making it Engaging:

Clear Explanations: Provide concise and clear explanations of each advanced feature, avoiding overly technical jargon.

Illustrative Examples: Use simple but effective examples to demonstrate the practical applications of these features.

Code Comparisons: Show how advanced features can lead to more concise or efficient code compared to basic approaches.

Real-World Use Cases: Discuss how these features are used in real-world Julia packages or applications.

Further Exploration: Provide links to relevant documentation or resources for readers who want to delve deeper into specific topics.

10.2 Contributing to the Julia Community

This chapter is where we inspire our readers to go beyond just using Julia and become active participants in its vibrant and growing community. Here's how we can guide them:

Why Contribute?

Giving Back: Explain that contributing to the Julia community is a way to give back to the open-source project that has empowered them with such a powerful tool.

Learning and Growth: Emphasize that contributing is an excellent way to deepen their understanding of Julia, improve their coding skills, and connect with other passionate Julia users.

Making a Difference: Highlight that even small contributions can make a significant impact on the Julia ecosystem and benefit countless other users.

Ways to Contribute

Improving Documentation:

Documentation Matters: Explain that clear and comprehensive documentation is crucial for any open-source project.

How to Contribute: Guide readers on how to improve existing documentation or add new documentation for packages or features.

Reporting Bugs:

Identifying and Reporting: Show how to identify and report bugs effectively, providing clear steps to reproduce the issue and relevant information.

Submitting Feature Requests:

Suggesting Improvements: Explain how to submit feature requests for Julia or its packages, providing clear descriptions and use cases.

Contributing Code:

Fixing Bugs or Adding Features: For more experienced users, guide them on how to contribute code by fixing bugs or adding new features to Julia or its packages.

The Pull Request Workflow: Explain the pull request workflow on GitHub for submitting code contributions.

Answering Questions and Helping Others:

Community Forums: Introduce community forums like the Julia Discourse forum and the Julia Slack channel where users can ask questions and help each other.

Sharing Knowledge: Encourage readers to share their knowledge and expertise by answering questions, providing guidance, and participating in discussions.

Creating Packages:

Expanding the Ecosystem: Explain how creating and sharing Julia packages can contribute to the growth and diversity of the Julia ecosystem.

Making it Engaging:

Success Stories: Share inspiring stories of individuals who have made significant contributions to the Julia community.

Community Spotlight: Highlight active members of the Julia community and their contributions.

Contribution Guides: Provide links to official contribution guides and resources for Julia and its packages.

Call to Action: Encourage readers to take the first step and make a contribution, no matter how small.

10.3 Further Resources and Learning

This final chapter serves as a springboard, propelling our readers to continue their Julia journey and explore the vast landscape of resources available. Here's how we can guide them:

Why Continue Learning?

The Journey Never Ends: Emphasize that learning is a continuous process, especially in a dynamic field like data science and with a rapidly evolving language like Julia.

Staying Ahead: Highlight the importance of staying up-to-date with the latest advancements, new packages, and best practices in the Julia ecosystem.

Expanding Horizons: Encourage readers to explore different areas of Julia and its applications, discovering new possibilities and expanding their skillset.

Resources for Further Learning

Official Julia Documentation:

The Primary Source: Emphasize the importance of the official Julia documentation as the most comprehensive and reliable source of information.

Specific Sections: Point out specific sections relevant to data science, such as the DataFrames.jl, Plots.jl, and machine learning documentation.

Online Courses and Tutorials:

Structured Learning: Recommend high-quality online courses and tutorials that provide structured learning paths for different levels and topics.

Platforms: Mention platforms like JuliaAcademy, Coursera, and YouTube channels with Julia content.

Books and Publications:

Deep Dives: Suggest books that delve deeper into specific aspects of Julia, such as advanced programming techniques, performance optimization, or specific application domains.

Community Forums and Resources:

Julia Discourse: Reiterate the value of the Julia Discourse forum for asking questions, seeking help, and engaging in discussions.

Julia Slack: Mention the Julia Slack channel for real-time interaction with other Julia users.

JuliaHub: Introduce JuliaHub as a platform for collaboration, package management, and accessing cloud resources.

Conferences and Meetups:

Connecting with the Community: Encourage readers to attend Julia conferences and meetups to connect with other Julia enthusiasts, learn from experts, and stay informed about the latest developments.

Making it Engaging:

Curated Resource List: Provide a curated list of recommended resources, categorized by topic or skill level.

Learning Paths: Suggest different learning paths based on readers' interests and goals.

Community Involvement: Encourage readers to join the Julia community, participate in discussions, and contribute to open-source projects.

Continuous Exploration: Inspire readers to stay curious, explore new packages and applications, and continue their Julia learning journey.